My Little book of Prayers

HAMLYN

London · New York · Sydney · Toronto

Talking to God

Dear God,
When I talk to my Mum or my Dad
I say things like
I love you
and . . .
Thank you
and . . .
I'm sorry
and . . .
Please.
You are my Father in Heaven.
So I'll talk to you
just as I talk to Mum or Dad.
I'll call you Heavenly Father.
You know my name.
So I'll just say

Love from Charlotte.

clare chaplin

Contents

Clare Chaplin

3

Published 1980 by
The Hamlyn Publishing Group Limited
London · New York · Sydney · Toronto
Astronaut House, Feltham, Middlesex, England
©Copyright 1980
The Hamlyn Publishing Group Limited.

Illustrations by
David Barnett
Corrine Burrows
Brian Bysouth
Gwen Green

ISBN 0 600 37261 8

Printed in Singapore by Tien Wah Press

Dear Heavenly Father,
You made everything –
   blue sky, twinkling stars,
   golden sun, silvery moon,
   green lands, blue seas.

You made all living things –
   birds and fish,
   plants and trees,
   animals and insects.
Best of all
you made people like me
to know you and love you.
How wonderful you are!

                    Love from *Charlotte*

Dear Heavenly Father,
You give us –
    the joy of spring,
        with golden flowers
        and songs of birds;
    the happiness of summer,
        with sunshine
        and holidays;
    the harvest of autumn,
        with fruits, vegetables
        and corn for bread;
    the fun of winter,
        with sparkling frost
        and cosy homes.
How good you are!

Love from *Charlotte*

Dear Heavenly Father,
You love all small things –
    little puppies and kittens,
    tiny birds in their nests,
    baby boys and girls.

You give them –
  Mums and Dads
  to care for them,
  cosy homes
  where they are warm and safe,
  good food
  to make them grow strong.
How loving you are!

Love from Charlotte

Dear Heavenly Father,
You give us
foods from the earth
and foods from the animals
to make us grow strong –
    crispy bread and cereals,
    green vegetables,
    gaily-coloured fruits,
    milk and butter and cheese,
    meat and fish,
    eggs and nuts,
    and water for our drinks.
How kind you are!

Love from 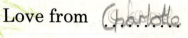 Charlotte

Dear Heavenly Father,
You gave me
    eyes to see,
    ears to hear,
    lips to speak and sing,
    hands to make and do,
    legs to walk and run.

Best of all
you gave me
    my mind to think,
    my heart to love.
Thank you for making me.

                    Love from *Charlotte*

Dear Heavenly Father,
Thank you for home –
  for Mum, for Dad,
  for brothers, for sisters,
  for friends, for pets.

Thank you for –
good food,
warm fires,
cosy beds,
toys and books and games.

Help me to thank you
for my home
by being kind and loving
to all my family.

Love from Charlotte.

Dear Heavenly Father,
Thank you for people
who care for us
and look after us –
   parents and teachers,
   policemen and shop-keepers,
   dustmen and road-sweepers,

doctors, dentists and nurses,
milkmen and postmen.
Help me to thank you
by caring for others
all I can.

Love from Charlotte

Dear Heavenly Father,
Thank you
for our animal friends and
for their gifts to us –
    milk from cows,
    eggs from hens,
    wool from sheep,
    songs from birds.
Thank you
for special pets
like dogs and cats.
Help me to be kind
to all our animal friends.

       Love from Charlotte

Dear Heavenly Father,
I know you love to forgive me
when I'm sorry.
I'm sorry if
    I do wrong,
    or hurt my pet,
    or quarrel with my friends.
I don't really want to be naughty,
especially if I hurt someone.
for then I'm sad.
Please help me to be good.

Love from Charlotte

Dear Heavenly Father,
Please forgive me
when I'm cross.
I get cross if I can't
do what I like
or
have what I want
or
get my own way.
I don't really want to be nasty,
especially if I'm unkind,
for then I'm unhappy.
Please help me to be good.

Love from .Charlotte.

Dear Heavenly Father,
You made us
to live together
in families –
  Mum, Dad,
  brothers, sisters,
  grandmas, grandpas,
  uncles, aunts, cousins.

Please take care of my family,
all those I love,
especially my friends.
Help us to live together happily
and to share with each other.

Love from Charlotte

Dear Heavenly Father,
Please take care of children who
    cannot see,
    cannot hear,
    cannot speak,
    cannot walk,
    children who are sick,
    children in hospital.

Bless those who look after them
with your loving care.
Help me never to be unkind
to children less fortunate
than myself.

Love from *Charlotte*

Dear Heavenly Father,
Please take care
of children, wherever they live,
who do not have
    clean water,
    enough food,
    good homes,
    proper schools,
    doctors and hospitals.
Bless those who work for them
and seek to help them.
Help us to share with others
the good things which we enjoy.

Love from *Charlotte*

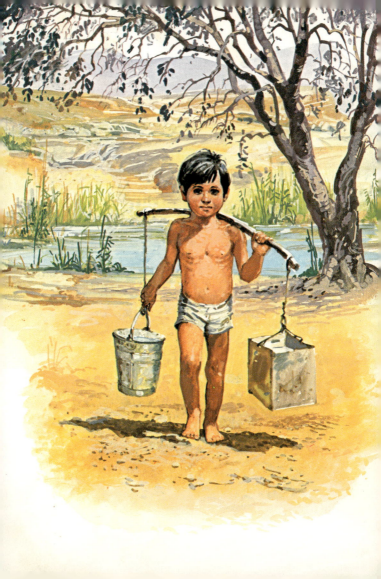

Dear Heavenly Father,
Please take care of
all our animal friends
and especially the pets we love.
Bless those who care for
    cats and dogs,
    horses and ponies,

sheep and cattle,
birds of the air.
Help me to be kind
to all living creatures and
especially to birds in winter.

Love from Charlotte

Dear Heavenly Father,
Once I was a baby,
now I'm a child,
one day I'll be grown up.
Help me to grow like you –
loving, and kind, and good.
Give me
    kind thoughts,
    kind words,
    kind deeds,
so that your love and goodness
may shine through me.

               Love from *Charlotte*

Dear Heavenly Father,
I see your beauty in flowers –
especially in their colours.
I see your beauty in Jesus –
especially in his goodness.
I see your beauty in people –
especially in their love.

Give me a loving heart
so that your beauty
may be seen in me.

Love from Charlotte

Dear Heavenly Father,
If I feel afraid
   make me brave.
If I feel cruel
   make me kind.
If I feel sad
   make me happy.
If I feel nasty
   make me loving.
If I want my own way
   make me think of others.

Then I shall become
more like you.

Love from *Charlotte*

Dear Heavenly Father,
You have given me everything –
    my life,
    my strength,
    my home,
    my friends.

Help me to give in return –
   my hands to be useful,
   my words to be kind,
   my feet to be helpful,
   my strength to be gentle,
   my heart to be loving.

             Love from *Charlotte*

Christmas

Dear Heavenly Father,
I love my birthday with
    my party,
    my presents,
    my cards.
I love the birthday of Jesus
on Christmas Day,
when we remember him with
    his parties,
    his presents,
    his cards.

Thank you for giving us
Jesus your Son,
the finest present of all,
on Christmas Day.

Love from Charlotte

Easter

Dear Heavenly Father,
I love the spring-time,
   when everything comes to life
   again after the death of winter.
In spring-time too comes Easter,
   when Jesus rose to life again
   after his death on the cross
   and lives for evermore.
May he always live in my heart.

Love from Charlotte

Clare Chaplin

Chape Clalin

Clr

Clane

Clane

Claure

Clane

Rev